www.finishinglinepress.com

The Shape of Home

poems by

Lee Chilcote

Finishing Line Press
Georgetown, Kentucky

The Shape of Home

ACKNOWLEDGMENTS

Many thanks to the editors of the following print and online journals in which these
poems were first published:

Roots Music: *Paddlefish*
Antoine: *Great Lakes Review*
Rites of Passage: *Blast Furnace*
Home Improvement: *Blue Bonnet Review*
In Medias Res: *Blue Bonnet Review*
The Edge of the World: *Pacific Review*
Shift Work: *Masque and Spectacle*
Color Line: *The Vermilion Literary Project*
Seen the Movie: *Gyroscope Review*

Two Fingers was awarded second place prize in the 2014 Lorain County Community
College poetry contest, and *Another Country* was a runner-up in the 2010 Poetry in the
Garden contest sponsored by the Baker-Nord Center for the Humanities at Case Western
Reserve University.

My sincere gratitude to the friends and colleagues who helped me navigate through this
project, and who supported me along the way: Brad Ricca, Susan Grimm, Nin Andrews,
David Hassler, Darlene Montonaro, and Meredith Holmes.

Many thanks to Kris Williams for the beautiful cover image. Love and eternal
thankfulness to my parents, and to my wife Katherine and my children Emily, Nathan and
Jonathan.

Publisher: Leah Maines
Editor: Christen Kincaid
Cover Art: Kris Williams
Author Photo: Tanya Rosen-Jones
Cover Design: Kris Williams

Printed in the USA on acid-free paper.
Order online: www.finishinglinepress.com
also available on amazon.com

Author inquiries and mail orders:
Finishing Line Press
P. O. Box 1626
Georgetown, Kentucky 40324
U. S. A.

Table of Contents

I.

Yet my attention still wandered
even though my eye remained stitched.

The Shape of Home

"In the fall of 1811, Horace Taylor and his wife (Nancy Douglass) accompanied the Spencer family to Claridon from Hartland, Connecticut."
—Claridon Congregational Church Record

The covered wagon rolling in
must have been a strange sight to the birds.
Except for a family of raccoons,
no one had lived in the cabin in years.
Leaves piled up against the threshold.

As he pulled on the reins,
the horses stamped the ground nervously.
Why had they climbed mountain switchbacks
crossed waist-deep rivers
for four thin walls that couldn't keep out the wind?
Night crowding in, howls deep in the forest.

He gathered wood to make the fire
but when his hands grew numb from the cold
he dropped the flint on the ground.

With his family huddled under a blanket,
he rode five miles to Burton
to borrow some flint and steel.
He stayed to warm his hands by the fire.

Arriving home after midnight,
he showered sparks on the kindling.
Light pushed the darkness away,
a sign of arrival.

Home Improvement

Every time you touch something it falls apart
says Dave the plumber
standing over a leaky set tub
that costs four hundred dollars to fix

He asks what I wanna do
and despite the field where a house was torn down
and home values in the shitter
I tell him go ahead

because I'm from Cleveland
where real estate is a place to live, a bubble
popped a long time ago

Things can only go up, we believe
but Dave, he does not believe in anything
his permanent scowl a warning to home owners everywhere

On Saturdays, we gather at Home Depot
an army of weekend warriors
rising up to replace shoe molding

Shift Work

After the kids go to sleep,
I rinse the dishes,
load them in the dishwasher
and crawl into bed.

Later, you'll come downstairs after falling asleep
in their beds, put the dishes away,
pack the bags for school
and curl up beside me.

In the night, we change diapers,
put crying kids back to bed,
tap each other's shoulders when we're too tired to get up,

make breakfast, feed the baby.
The clang of another soccer game,
another trip to the grocery store.
The slip-slop rhythm of us.

Then we go out on weekends,
skip the appetizers, skip the desserts, skip the movie.
Walk hand in hand past the twentysomethings

to go home and make love,
voicing our gratitude
for clocking in, for showing up,
for cradling each other in the dark,
two bodies at rest
until the baby cries at 3 a.m.

Alchemy

The staples in my family
were frozen burgers, white rice
and bland blocks of orange cheese.
Dinner a sacred half-hour no one escaped
until we mopped our plates.

Mom barely let us open the cupboards
without a chaperone.

Living with a friend after college,
I learned to cook in a galley kitchen.
Too broke to go out
I discovered pesto, Camembert, cumin,

made pasta with red pepper
and vodka cream sauce,
veggie curry, pepper jack burritos
and ate paella, rice noodles and peanut sauce
while sipping two buck chuck.

Lazy Eye

My left eye rolled off like a foul ball
among the dandelions,

squirted like a fish
out of my hands into the lake,

careened like a pea
under the dining room table,

wandered 'til the world became blurry
and my sight skipped

like an old TV on the fritz.
Bright lights, big people.

My parents smiling and waving at me.
Look at me, my mother said.

And I did, my sight clear, but soon
my eye wandered off again—

beamed like a gutter ball
off to the side,

bounced like a rubber ball
into a storm drain,

sauntered like a stray
across lanes of traffic.

Need to get a collar for that thing.
Keep it inside.

When I was three, my mother took me to see Dr. Price
who said that I needed *an operation.*
My eye was lazy, he said.

After my operation
I woke up groggy, but my eye stayed put.
The nurses gave me Jell-O.

I held my mother's hand on the way to preschool
and said hi and bye to her friends.
Yet my attention still wandered
even though my eye remained stitched.

Then the dog
became Baryshnikov,
the linoleum floor
an ice rink,
the front hall
a race track …

I leveled tall mountains and
turned sand into civilizations.

I kept my eye tucked in my pocket
until it was safe to bring it out.

Promise Me to Speak from Your Heart

We ride through Rockefeller Park
our shadows like birds playing in the sky
under old stone bridges
a fresco of sky and trees

to lie beneath an old oak.
Flowers to choose, invitations to send.
When spring comes, we'll say our vows.

Do you, Katherine,
of the shambling, crazy-roommate apartment on Derbyshire
take this man Lee
who bummed a ride when his car wouldn't start
to have and to hold
for richer, for poorer
filtering all important news from the Daily Show
till death do you part?

These vows say nothing
of how our hearts fit together
like puzzle pieces from the same box.

Two Fingers

You brought a black girl home to jump rope:
holding hands and chanting
as you skipped along the drive.
When grandpa got home from the hospital, your head flew
above the fence,
red pigtails flopping
beside her black braids.
He climbed the steps and slammed the door.

When he got sick and moved in,
I carried cereal and orange juice to his room,
his back bent from polio, his voice
a whisper.

He watched the Derby in a starched shirt
and powder blue sweater,
holding up two fingers for whiskey.
He sat next to me on the couch
and helped me pick a winner, then leaned forward
and shook his cane
as his horse thundered around the track.

When I climbed the stairs to say goodnight
I tried to reconcile your stories
about train rides to see his family in Texas
and house calls he made after church
with the banished girl.
He smelled like Old Spice and his stubbly
cheek grazed mine
as I reached up to hold him tight.

Where I Write

On envelopes, napkins, backs of bills,
in the grocery store line,
at red lights until the cars start honking,
in the garden, my hands caked in dirt,
at my desk, avoiding eye contact with the to-do list,
at the playground, tapping a poem between cartwheels,
my muses are sirens, trains, barking dogs,
the slide where someone wrote 'fuck you,'
the flowers Vicky planted before losing the house,
the library where five-year-olds climb in my lap,
at cocktail parties, pretending to listen to vacation stories,
in bed, until I can't keep my eyes open,
in the morning
seed-bombing words into the cracks and crevices.

Antoine

Up before dawn, I trudged through snowdrifts
to the barn where he slept in hay.
Hearing my footsteps and the rattle of the gate
he charged me on quivering legs.
I pulled the bottle from my coat
and he tackled me, nibbling my fingers and sleeves
as if this was his last meal.

Our class arrived in Vermont as strangers
yet soon our lives were knit together
sweeping crap out of the turkey barn,
splitting logs in the wood lot
and digging potatoes up on Garden Hill.

Poetry had always been my rusty fire escape.
Yet here, beneath a dome of stars,
I couldn't write a thing.

Our teacher invited us to hear David Budbill
who wrote about a French-Canadian woodcutter in Judevine.
When he finished, I asked if he had any advice
and he told me keep writing, no matter what.
Maybe I'd get published in obscure journals
read by a handful of people—mostly librarians—
and I'd never have any money, but I'd be happy.

That winter the calves were weaned.
My roommate Jeremy and I named ours Antoine
after the burly logger in Budbill's poems.
As my forty-pound toddler pitched towards me
I thought about the life waiting at home
reading Shakespeare and wearing khakis
while he trotted off to the slaughterhouse
to feed the students next spring.

In Medias Res

I arrived late to the party
after the food was cold and half-eaten
after the hosts who were half-drunk
had become half-sober
in the middle of stories
about things that happened before I was born

Late to kindergarten
I swung open the metal doors
dropped in
a trumpet blast in a measure of rest
Late to the playground
my own shoes
walked off without me

Late to the restaurant
where my date drank alone
to the office meeting
where they decided my future
to church on Sunday
where grace drifted onto my shoulders

When I finally arrived
my voice appeared like a glass of champagne
at the party I was missing
my paper getting an A+
my mouth full of baubles
my hips sinking into the soft nest
between her thighs

On time the gray hairs of whiskers
sprouted on my cheeks
and children sprang forth
like sunflowers
I hoisted them up to see my kingdom
lining up my mistakes like milk jugs

Too soon they stared at me
blank as new odometers
and climbed onto my shoulders
where they rode like prom kings and queens
into the future
devouring life in great gulps of air

II.

Love lifts you off your feet
then dumps you in the broken-tiled foyer.

Roots Music

The needle hit the record
and through the scratchy silence came a sandpaper voice,
the wallop of a backbeat,
the fat notes of electric guitar.

We kicked the rug back from the hardwood floors
and Dad tipped his head back and crooned.
His forehead beaded
as he played the air harp
with his eyes closed.

Senior year in high school he borrowed his dad's car,
picked up his friends and drove
to a joint on Euclid
with glass block windows and a neon sign.
Driving down Cedar Hill was like opening a door
to the life he'd always known about
through the fuzzy AM radio.

He stood shoulder to shoulder with black kids
listening to Lightnin' Slim.
When the lights came up, the crowd spilled into the street.
Dad and his white friends lit cigarettes
and stole glances from their Buick.
As the parking lot emptied out, the last few
blue notes shivered down his spine.

When he said that, on the record Lightnin' moaned,
the harmonica wailed
and Dad and I hit the floor
hard enough that the record skipped—
Mom calling from the kitchen,
shaking off her soapy hands
what's goin' on out there?

Circling David

After 'David' by Michelangelo

He towers above me,
a porch light we flutter into,
contrapposto form,
hand curling into a fist.

I got no sleep
on the overnight train.
Loud Italian voices spilled
from the next cabin.

They passed a bottle
in the hallway, hot with laughter while
I stayed
rubbing words in the dark.

Now,

       his fingers thick as rope,
       sling hanging off his back like nothing.

Now,

       his piercing eyes,
       veins bulging from his wrists.

Now,

       his shoulders
       beneath a garland of hair.

Two-Dollar Red

A fat old man with one blind eye totters up behind the bar.
We ask for a tasting
and he pours his favorite, a Cab Franc.
I stare at his eye, a milky-white orb.

He tells us about Konstantin Frank
who had learned to grow grapes and make red wine
where a foot of snow is a dusting
and summer doesn't start until after the Fourth.

"I've just turned ninety-three
and the secret to my longevity is drinking
red wine every day," he says.

We'll drink to that, ordering two bottles.
The old man opens one and fills our glasses.

"To our health," you say, clinking them together
to celebrate our first anniversary,
the two-dollar red we've guzzled,
the mouth-feel of the moment.

Seen the Movie

When I was eight or nine
I asked my father if he'd killed anyone in Vietnam.
He shook his head.

"We didn't see much action," he said.
I pictured men in camouflage
playing poker and looking at girlie mags, like on TV.

Did you ever get shot?

Dad thought a minute.
"There was one time.
I was pinned against a tree.
There was a guy shooting at me
and I couldn't go anywhere."

So, what happened?
"He ran out of bullets."

My dad, who captained a platoon at 24,
had five or six stories like that,
all of them PG.

On Friday nights, he watched war movies,
beer bottles stacking up in the sink.
As the credits rolled, we crawled over him.

Is that what it was like, Daddy?
"Not really," he said.

At the Boston Aquarium

Penguins waddle across the rocks,
jump in and shoot
through the water like missiles.
You laugh as I hold you up to see.

The naturalist in a wetsuit
explains how they shed their feathers.
The process takes a few weeks.
Catastrophic molting, it's called.

First, they gorge themselves
and then fast for a while.
Feathers fall out and new ones poke through
like a bad haircut,

like after being up at 3 a.m.
you run to me the next day and we fly through the air.
You clutch my two-day beard
and shout "Again! Again!"

Rock 'n' Rollers

One morning we were
playing in the yard when
my oldest brother Don
flung open the screen door
carrying a boom box. It
was freshly loaded with
a set of eight D batteries.
He set it down on the
driveway and pressed play:
Listen, he commanded.
"Hurt So Good" leapt out
of the speakers and he
began jerking around like a
possessed pogo stick. When
Johnny Cougar shouted
"*Hey!*" we all started gyrating
our hips like Elvis. We spent
afternoons watching MTV,
smooth-chested ten or
eleven-year-old boys
learning about sex from
guys with long hair who
wore tight pants and makeup.

Caveat Emptor

Love only takes you so far
before you stare at the stranger in the dark
you're sleeping with.

It keeps you under its spell for years
until one day you wake
and see her white foot like a sandbar,
your clothes on the floor,
and picture the car keys in the bowl downstairs.

Love lifts you off your feet
and dumps you with the dust bunnies
in the broken-tiled foyer,
breaks down by the side of the road,
folds like a Ponzi scheme.

When you're tired and the kitchen's a mess,
love is on the sofa
binge-watching Netflix.

She is the architect who shrugs her shoulders
when cracks start to show
and the house begins to slide downhill.

Extras

After 'Frieze of Dancers' by Edgar Degas

After some TV and whining
Emily puts on her leotard.
We arrive as the class is starting.
Four-year-olds bounce around at the barre,
watching themselves in the mirror.
Miss Donna charms them into brief poses—
first position, second position, nice job girls!—
as parents snap pictures on their iPhones,
chatting about the cost of ballet slippers.

At home, Emily puts on a princess dress
and a Disney's Greatest Hits CD
as Nathan runs laps.
I scrape play-dough off the carpet.
You clean up the pancakes from breakfast.

Mean Boys

Playfighting in the yard with three-year-old Nathan,
he lunges at me and our sticks cross.
Then he takes a break to finish his popsicle.

"How was school today?"
"Oh-kay."
"What happened?"
"The kids were mean to me."

Nathan is a smooth plank of muscle
who towers over the other preschoolers.
Yet the mean boys hide in the bathroom,
spilling out when the lights are off.

Wiping his sticky mouth on his sleeve,
he forgets all about them.
He yells "Hi-yah!" and slashes my leg.
I fall down with a campy groan
and he jumps on me, grinning.

I hug his puffed-out chest and bruised knees
until he wriggles free.

"Let's go read stories."
"I can jump on a trampoline with one foot."
He's still punching the air
as I reach for his hand.

I Carry the Booze

Beer ran down the basement steps
in a foamy river of suds
and sprang from the garden hose
like a geyser of piss
and leaked from the fridge
until the floor was sticky like flypaper
and froze into icicles
that hung from the gutters like stalactites.

What beer? We said.
What icicles melting in the sun?
Sucking on them like candy.

We poured beer over the turkey
like grandma's gravy
and served Miller with straws
at my sister's Hello Kitty birthday party
and hid six packs of the good stuff under the tree
and spent our spring break
on a float trip down a river of booze.

The word was always omitted
like a library book with a page ripped out.
It only appears in hindsight,
a negative in the carousel of memory.

The fight over car keys,
the ride home in a roller coaster
that had swerved off its tracks.
The men swaying like palm trees
as we said good night.
Late night football in the foyer,
mom shouting like a referee.

When I had my first drink
it was like pouring gasoline on a bonfire.
I walked into parties with beer
in my shoes.

"You look like you need a drink,"
someone said with a grin,
handing me a fresh beer.

When I met my wife
she was as booze-soaked as I was,
drunks sleeping it off
in all the branches of her family tree.

To kiss her, I drank two beers.
I was sober when we made love
except for the bourbon in my veins.

In the morning sun,
her heart was like driftwood
stripped clean and bare by the ocean.

Now I wake up each day
and pour milk on my cereal
and drink two cups of coffee.
Yet I see a cold foamy draft
in the sun-streaked wood floor
and beer in the light bulbs
and there's beer in my bones
from before I was born.

III.

But we went anyway,
the curtain of trees closed behind us.

The Edge of the World

The muddy, shale-bottomed stream
filled with sewage after a hard rain
and mom said we couldn't go there
because that's where they hid the bodies.
But we went anyway,
the curtain of trees closed behind us,
the traffic above us a whisper.
We lit firecrackers and told jokes.

1979. Black families swam upstream into
our pure white suburb.
We met them in kindergarten classes and on the playground
and played until our mothers called us home.

Doan Brook flowed through leafy gorges
before running underground and dumping into Lake Erie.
In our four-block world, it was in the ravine
the cops had found headless nurses,
old stone bridges crumbled
and the water was always empty of fish.

One day we defied our parents and walked the stream
as far as we could.
Where the trail ended, it plunged
into a cesspool of sticks and trash.
Then it entered a tunnel four feet high
and disappeared into darkness.

My brother said he was going inside.
For a moment after he stepped in the tunnel,
stooping to fit in its slimy concrete maw,
we couldn't see him anymore.
He'd stepped off the edge of the world.
Came out with a grin and foul-smelling shoes.

Butterflies

I'm jealous you can feel her moving
so I talk to her in bed,
imagining what she looks like—
half-moon fingernails, downy hair.

You squeeze the pillow and twist the sheets,
your belly like a downward dog,
wrinkled end of a balloon.

As you drift off
with your back to me,
I lie awake and stare into the dark.

Are we ready?
How will our lives be different?
Outside, nothing's changed
yet as the day ticks closer,
I feel dread.

You grab my hand: *Here.*
She kicks like a swimmer,
the world a chrysalis.

Living in Captivity

Driving the kids to school with Barney in my ear, I begin to feel like I'm a captive on Kid Island. I haven't listened to NPR in a week and suddenly miss hearing about the stock market, the Supreme Court and Pluto. I used to listen to NPR all the time: Morning Edition, All Things Considered, Fresh Air and late night jazz. I stayed awake to find out who would be president in 2000 and learned about derivatives and mortgage-backed securities when I lost my real estate job. Now I'll catch maybe 45 seconds before the kids interrupt me. Last night, there was a segment on Cuban soul music as I was pulling into the driveway. I eased the mini-van into the garage, holding my ear to the speaker to catch the end of it. As soon as the car stopped, the kids started screaming like prisoners in their seat belts: "*Daaad, I want to get out!*" I glared at them and shook my finger in the rearview mirror. "*One more minute!*" But it was already on to the weather.

Color Line

Arms poking out the windows,
the bus rumbled past ivy-
draped mansions and sagging doubles
to the Cleveland Museum of Art's
white pillars perched on a hill.

Inside, we wanted to kick off our shoes
and slip-slide on the marble floors,
ride the banisters, but our teachers' looks warned us off.

We followed like ducklings to "Stag at Sharkey's"
by George Bellows. One boxer curled his fist
grappling with another one in the ring
and men with lurid faces egged them on.

In a room full of European masters,
the nudes made the boys titter and the girls gasp:
Cupid slipped from Psyche's bed
wearing nothing but a grin,
not even a leaf, and left her there.

When we reached the armor court at last,
the boys kicked and punched each other,
being bold in battle.

We rode the bus back up the hill,
shaken together like oil and vinegar,
the bus driver yelling at us to sit back down.

The Greatest Guitarist of All Time

My brother's band played AC/DC and Led Zeppelin
to groupies in the school gym
who cheered them on
by card tables filled with Coke bottles.
I longed to be the Plant to his Page, the Jagger to his Richards,
but instead they chose John Meyer.

Seventies hard rock shook our house's Spanish plaster
so I bought an Alvarez acoustic guitar
and learned all of Bob Dylan's Greatest Hits, Volume II,
singing it through my nose:
"Aw, momma, can this really be the eeeeend?"

"I hope so!" Mike yelled.

One day, I climbed onstage
and sang backup into a mic left on in the corner
when his band was playing at a lunchtime school concert.
I even did Axl Rose's snake dance during "Sweet Child of Mine."
Afterwards, Mike wouldn't even talk to me.

Now we get together at the playground,
pushing our kids on the swings
as we argue about who's the greatest guitarist of all time.

Another Country

"This is why Ireland is so green," you say as rain blots out the windshield while we're driving around the Ring of Kerry. A Volvo doing eighty roars past us as the road straightens. I hit the gas and you clutch the seat and scream: "Aaaah!"

"If it's the buses or the ditch, I'll take the buses."

"Is that supposed to make me feel *better*?"

The only sound is the slap of wipers after that. The past few months have been a blur of wedding plans being sewn up. Now it's just us, sudden occupants of the life we've planned.

We pull off in a speck of a town. At the pub we order Guinness and argue about where to go next. The tarted-up girls nod their approval when we play Pogues, U2 and the Clash on the jukebox. As drunks start chanting football songs, we realize we're the only ones not singing.

On the way back to the car, we stop at a fish and chip shop. We devour fried cod wrapped in butcher paper and talk about missing Starbucks, juicy cheeseburgers.

At the hotel, we make love as wind knocks against the window and a car alarm goes off. I lie awake in the dark. Perhaps marriage is not a home, but a home-leaving—an imperfect residence in another's soul.

Catching Sunfish

I spent all day in the sun,
feet dangling off the dock,
catching one after another
then hauled my bucket to the porch.

Can we eat them? I asked.
They were only about the size of my hand.
Fishermen threw them back.

Mom got out a knife
and spread newspapers on the counter.
She plucked out a golden beauty
and sawed off its head.

I watched in horror
as its severed mouth gulped for air
before—finally—growing still.

Wearing her vacuum face,
Mom scooped out the guts
and trimmed the skin.
A silver dollar of meat, our prize.

Veni Vidi Vici

When I open the fridge on Thursday
a week's groceries have disappeared
as if a troop of Roman soldiers came, saw and conquered,
leaving behind only boot prints.

Twenty dollar bills slough off the minute we leave the house.
Stopping at the store for toilet paper,
the kids scream for Barbie and Spiderman.
I whisk them past the toys asleep in shiny boxes.

I ask my mom to patch the holes in the kids' pants,
new a month ago.
I used to cringe at the hand-me-downs.
Yet now I respect her bin of lost buttons,
her sewing table.

Home from school,
the kids devour a carton of raspberries,
shoving them in their mouths,
their faces and hands red as blood-stained cherubs.

I put the rest away
but they make a break for it.
Climb in the fridge, pull down yogurt,
scale the cabinets and topple teddy grahams.
Eat right off the floor.

Because You Said We're Like Roommates

As I walked you home, we kept talking
our shoulders brushing together
past the Winking Lizard where voices spilled into the street
everything in black and white except us
floating above the sidewalk
you asked me in
we sat on the couch and I thought about the moves I'd make
you turned on the Daily Show
I touched your leg and you didn't move away
during the interview we held hands
the credits rolled, you smiled and tipped your head

On Friday nights, we lie in bed and watch Netflix
catching up
tomorrow there's tumbling class and cleaning the house
we need toilet paper
I turn off the lights and start kissing you
after going down on you
I slip inside you
flames climb the curtains
engulfing the room
we lie there breathless, say "I love you"
and fall asleep

Rites of Passage

Catholics have transubstantiation
but Protestants have fathers who
only appear at night
to brush their foreheads,
then one day when you're five or seven
you bump into them in the hallway
like a tall wisp of smoke.

I first saw my father in daylight
when I got up to deliver the newspapers on our street.
Trudging downstairs half-awake,
I found him in the kitchen
eating a bowl of cheerios.

The room reeked of aftershave
like a priestly incense.
He looked up and smiled at me,
offered words of encouragement
then drove off in his Cutlass Supreme.

Seeing Dad with the sports section
like a unicorn in a sudden clearing
made getting up worthwhile.

I absorbed the hyperbolic font
as I stuffed papers in my sack,
a spring
in the machine of the world.

Lee Chilcote lives in a 1900 Victorian in Cleveland, Ohio with his wife, Katherine, and their three children. He has worked as a community organizer, real estate developer, writer and teacher. He attended Middlebury College, Lincoln College at Oxford University, and Cleveland State University, where he obtained a master's degree in English and Creative Nonfiction and was awarded the Leonard Trawick Prize for Creative Writing.

Chilcote is a journalist, essayist and poet. His articles have appeared in *Vanity Fair, Next City, Belt, Planning, Land and People* and numerous other publications. His poetry and creative nonfiction have been published by *Great Lakes Review, Pacific Review, Oyez Review* and others. His essays have appeared in the books *Rust Belt Chic: A Cleveland Anthology, The Cleveland Neighborhood Guidebook,* and *A Race Anthology.*

He serves as executive director of the nonprofit Literary Cleveland, whose mission is to create and nurture a vibrant literary arts community in Northeast Ohio.

CPSIA information can be obtained
at www.ICGtesting.com
Printed in the USA
LVOW12s1447250417
532119LV00002B/529/P